ERASING DANGEROUS

FAULT LINES

FROM VICTIM TO VICTOR

ERASING DANGEROUS
FAULT LINES

FROM VICTIM TO VICTOR

FRANK A. JONES, III

HUNTER ENTERTAINMENT NETWORK
Colorado Springs, Colorado

Erasing Dangerous Fault Lines, From Victim to Victor
Copyright © 2024 by Dr. Frank A. Jones, III
First Edition: September 2024

All rights reserved. No part of this book may be reproduced or transmitted in any form or by any means without written permission of the publisher, except in brief quotes or reviews. Unless otherwise noted, all Scripture is taken from the King James Version of the Bible (KJV). All rights reserved. Used by permission.

To order products, or for any other correspondence:

Hunter Entertainment Network
Colorado Springs, Colorado 80840
www.hunter-ent-net.com
Tel. (253) 906-2160
E-mail: contact@hunter-entertainment.com
Or reach us on Facebook or Instagram at: Hunter Entertainment Network
"Offering God's Heart to a Dying World"

This book and all other Hunter Entertainment Network™ Hunter Heart Publishing™, and Hunter Heart Kids™ books are available at Christian bookstores and distributors worldwide.

Book cover design: Phil Coles Independent Design
Layout & logos: Exousia Marketing Group www.exousiamg.com

ISBN (Paperback): 979-8-3303-5382-8
ISBN (eBook): 979-8-3303-5383-5

Printed in the United States of America..

Dedication

I would like to dedicate this book to my community of love and support. First, to my mother Elizabeth Ann Jones who has been a pillar of grace and hope. My father, the late Frank Jones, Jr. who taught me valuable lessons of life. My wife, Felisha Nelson Jones whose love and support gives me inspiration and encouragement daily. My amazing kids Raven, Stephen, and Bryanna who illuminate my life and bring me great joy and a sense of accomplishment with all their success. My precious parents in Love, Pastor James and Loretta Nelson who embraced me as their own and showed me unmitigated love. My spiritual parents in the faith, Bishop Raymond Johnson and Sis Mildred Johnson, HRM King Drolor Bosso Adante I and Lady Martha.

Acknowledgments

I would like to acknowledge the staff and members of the *City of Refuge Church* whom I have had the privilege and honor to oversee the past 24 years. I am the man that I am having been blessed with the opportunity to serve you.

Publisher and Author, Deborah G. Hunter and Hunter Entertainment Network publishing company for capturing and running with the vision.

And our friends, Pastor Cross and Louis Richard.

Table of Contents

Chapter 1

Hidden Fault Lines

1

Hidden Fault Lines

"Therefore judge nothing before the time, until the Lord come, who both will bring to light the hidden things of darkness, and will make manifest the counsels of the hearts: and then shall every man have praise of God." 1 Corinthians 4:5

Our lives are the sum total of relationships. Our relationships with our parents, siblings, colleagues, church family, and yes, our God, is critical for healthy living. Relationships are designed to enhance, sharpen, support, encourage, and assist. Our God created us in a way whereby we are a part of God's supernatural ecosystem. Such that no man or woman is an island and we need each other in order to maximize who we are.

There was a popular Gospel song in the 90's which stated, "As long as I've got King Jesus, I don't need nobody else." Though this song was popular at the time, it was not scripturally accurate. We need one another. The child that says to their father, "I don't need you," or even the spouse to his or her partner, deprives themselves of the power that is locked in these covenant relationships. Just because these relationships are full of potential, does not mean they will not encounter rough patches or common disagreements. A fault is formed in the Earth's crust as a brittle response to **stress**.

Many relationships today are being built upon what I consider to be *hidden fault lines*. These fault lines periodically reveal the tremors and even earthquakes. And as with natural earthquakes, we hold on until the shaking passes. Then, we assess the damage and move on until the next one occurs. Though we know this is negligence, we sacrifice our safety and peace for temporary comfort.

For example, the San Andreas fault is one of the most famous and dangerous faults in North America. It is believed to span 1200 Kilometer (750 miles) through California. Movies have been made giving reference to the so-called big one that geologists say, God forbid, has the potential to occur. With each earthquake, the potential for this to occur intensifies. Yet thousands migrate to California annually because of the appeal of such a beautiful State. There have been numerous earthquakes throughout the years. Some see this as a warning that seismologists say will come true.

We can see this example pertaining to relationships that have settled for surface, vain images of success rather than experiencing victory within and without.

In our relationships, we all have been, or will be in, one of two positions. We will be the forgiver or the forgiven. We will be the offender or the offended and yes, the aggressor or the victim. These positions change depending upon certain circumstances. These positions and the conduct can be an asset or a liability to you in life. Mastering each position is essential for a healthy relationship that will promote our Christ.

In each case, we will receive, lay blame, or even fault on the other part whether it is valid or not. But in order to live a life free of the consequences of fault finding, we must be willing to accept personal responsibility for our own actions and feelings.

My prayer is that this book will give you the tools to walk in victory by erasing *hidden fault lines* in relationships regardless of what type.

Chapter 2

Root Causes and Invisible Fault Lines

2

Root Causes and Invisible Fault Lines

"But you should say, why persecute him, seeing the **root of the matter** is found in me?" Job 19:28

Offenses and finger pointing is common whenever there is a disagreement. Whoever believes they are the victim, or that there is a deficiency in a relationship, shifts the blame or points the finger to someone else. "My condition is not my fault" is often the thinking of most people. It's the government, the minorities, the powerful, and yes even the devil that has placed me in this situation. When in all actuality, the power to heal and succeed resides within us all.

God has given us the ability to achieve success and peace, but it is His way, not ours. Fallen man does not look in the mirror but focuses on external powers to be the reason for his/her demise. Remember that even our salvation is a product of us acknowledging and confessing that we are sinners and our position changes when we repent (change our minds). Victory occurs when we win from within.

Our text reveals a very common situation in life when it comes to those who are closest to us. In this case, his three friends: Eliphaz, Bildad, and Zophar come to comfort him but rather justify his actions based upon their personal analysis. Doesn't this seem common today how that a person's true feelings regarding your plight is revealed during your lowest moment? Attempting to accurately identify the problem, we should never inspect the fruit alone but true understanding comes when we know the root, or source, of the problem. Every effect has a root cause which is often hidden in plain sight.

"He that answereth a matter before he heareth it, it is folly and shame unto him" Proverbs 18:13.

Instructions are given when dealing with an uncomfortable dilemma in a relationship, and the consequences of not hearing the whole matter. Two derogatory terms are used to describe the person who provides an answer with all the facts. The first being **folly** which means:

1. Lacking good sense.
2. A foolish act, idea, or practice.
3. An ornamental building with no practical purpose

The Bible identifies this individual as such. How often have we felt like a fool because we have made a decision based upon partial information, or even misinformation? The results of such are found in the second word: **shame**, meaning a feeling of worthlessness, which is the effect of an inadequate response.

In order to assist and be a resource in any relationship, it is incumbent upon us to patiently get to the root of the matter.

I heard a story once of a young woman who was experiencing excruciating pain, which required the attention of a specialist. While on her visit, she was asked what was wrong and where she was hurting? She then replied to the physician and said, "I hurt all over!" The physician proceeded to ask her to touch certain areas of her anatomy with her index finger. He asked her to touch her knee with her index finger and she responded, "Yes, it hurts there."

Next, he asked her to touch her chest with the same finger. She replied, "Yes, it hurts there." Lastly, he asked her to touch her head and as you guessed, she said that it hurt there, as well. After a very thorough examination, the woman anxiously asked the question, "Doctor, what's wrong with me?" He looked at her and responded, "You have a dislocated index finger!" She assumed, as many of us would, that her pain was the sign of a fatal disease. Assuming the worst, she analyzed the fruit and never considered the root.

Just like the woman with the finger, Job's friends were the finger that needed to be healed before they could give comfort during a time of need. If we are going to be a friend, spouse, citizen, or even Christian, we must first perform introspection before we can accurately give counsel to the hurting. Our own personal *fault lines* can influence our perspective.

These fault lines remain dormant for a season but can then shift without notice, causing there to be an earthquake of inaccurate counsel. Emotional trauma, past hurts, and unattended wounds can fester and become lethal for relationships. Thus as Job replied, *the root of the matter is within you.*

Just as the root or foundation, faulty fault lines are not sufficient to build upon and must be addressed before progress can be made. Just like the root fault lines produce certain reactions or earthquakes such as anger, violence, wrath, and depression when certain triggers occur.

Chapter 3

Bitter Roots and Toxic Fruit

3

Bitter Roots and Toxic Fruit

"Follow peace with all men, and holiness, without which no man shall see the Lord. Looking diligently lest any man fail of the grace of God; lest any root of bitterness springing up trouble you, and thereby many be defiled."
Hebrews 12:14, 15

One example of a faulty root system can be found in Hebrews 12:14,15. The writer of the Book of Hebrews, which many credit to the Apostle Paul, gives important instructions. First, he directs us to follow, or seek, peace with everyone. If you are like me, the older I get, the more I enjoy peace. Many have withdrawn from certain relationships because they set a premium on peace of mind. He tells us to pursue two things: *peace and holiness* and the potential blindness that will occur as it relates to seeing God if we don't. Another translation says *make every effort or work at living in peace with everyone.* But the work begins within.

"There can be not potent and fruitful outreach until there is serious in reach"

Now, He commands us to take personal inventory and look diligently within and without. As a watchman is perched on a watchtower, so we ought to watch and look diligently for ourselves and others.

"As every man hath received the gift, even so minister the same one to another as good stewards of the manifold grace of God" 1 Peter 4:10.

The potential to fail, which means to fall from, come short, and come late in regards to His grace, is possible when we neglect to follow these instructions. Then, according to Hebrews 12:15, *the root of bitterness* springs up, troubles you, and defiles others.

Just like the fault lines, the root of bitterness can have far reaching catastrophic results, causing you trouble and defiling others.

"Bitterness is unmitigated anger that has been seeded by hurt, fertilized, and irrigated by carnal counsel, selfish, and ignorant ideals."

The *root of bitterness* embraces anger and faults others for emotional, economic, and spiritual conditions. And though these feelings can be justified, they can only lead to paralysis and stagnation. The root of bitterness is a *poisonous root* that causes you to scowl. Yes, even the demeanor of the person who allows bitterness to seed is visible. One translation describes the root of bitterness to be a poisonous root. Not only does it make you and those you associate yourself with sick, but it can also be lethal.

The fruit of the root of bitterness can be seen in other expressions, as well. Bitter people are harsh, critical, hard to get along with, judgmental, sarcastic, filled with anger, and sometimes passive aggressive.

Once again, imagine Job's conversation with his three friends and what he was actually saying concerning their attempt to assist him. *The root of the matter is in you!* Yes, the root cause is evident. We see them finding fault in Job rather than praying and seeking God to remove the root within themselves.

Notice that the writer is specifically writing to the people of God. You ask how this can be? Again, I will say it is when hurt is allowed time to seed and germinate. Therefore, within the Church, we have bitter brothers, sour sisters, and as one great man of God says, *caustic Christians*. This hinders the flow of the Spirit in relationships of all kinds. These can never experience their full potential because the root of bitterness has caused a fault line. This fault line is hidden in plain sight. Again, we will never go to the next level in our relationships until we pull down strongholds, uproot bitterness, and erase dangerous fault lines.

This is possible through the direction of the Holy Spirit and the power of the Word of God.

The Bible exposes the symptoms as well as the root causes of most depression, isolation, and contentiousness, and through spiritual diagnosis, we have discovered that there is a fault line caused by the root of bitterness. But let me say by the end of this book, you will walk in victory because the Father will show you how to overcome past hurts, and live the way He has purposed for you and your family. Yes, you have a right to be free! And I am determined to see you free and flourishing in every relationship that you are engaged in.

Why don't you stop for a moment and confess that "I have a right to be free!!!" How liberating that statement is. How powerful it is to know your Kingdom rights. Truly, through the Anointed One and His anointing, we are free indeed! No more chains. No more fault lines.

"Bitterness is a choice which results in the negative response of the offended."

Chapter 4

Sour Patches and Lemon Heads

4

Sour Patches and Lemon Heads

"Either make the tree good, and his fruit good; or else make the tree corrupt, and his fruit corrupt: for the tree is known by his fruit." Matthew 12:33

Growing up in the South in a small community, we were blessed to have what was called *sweet shops*. These were small shops that kept inexpensive candy. They catered to young people. And many times, I believe they were not there for profit but rather to minister to the youth. Our community had quite a few. Once, I was provoked to try something new.

Yes, as you may have imagined, it was *lemonheads* and a candy called *sour patches*. It didn't take long after one taste for me to know, or my friends to know, I didn't like them. The shriveling expression on my face told the whole story. I had just tasted something that was Bitter! And I learned early to be prepared for that taste.

As with the candy, bitter people don't smile but rather frown. They are toxic from the root. And anyone that tastes of their fruit becomes as they are. Satan has a lot of hurting people infected by the discontent and bitterness of others. As with the pandemic, this disease is contracted through contact. If you're not protected, you will be infected!

The Bible clearly says that a *good tree has good fruit and a corrupt tree has corrupt fruit.* That is how you identify a tree— by its fruit. I would say the fruit of the tree reveals its root. Whether it is rooted in love or hate.

"So that Christ may dwell in your hearts by faith; that ye, being rooted and grounded in love," Ephesians 3:17.

Good fruit begins in the heart and is expressed in words and kind deeds. Corrupt and bitter fruit begin in the heart and also manifests in words and actions. Thus, becoming an issue that can affect your community, workplace, homelife, and even ministry experience. We not only taste its juices, but we also share it with others.

"Be not deceived: evil communications corrupt good manners" 1 Corinthians 15:33.

Being in a toxic environment with bitter people can alter your behavior. And though you are good with pure intentions, their communication can and will infect you. The root of the word communicate is "commune." This means to live together sharing possessions. *Homeleo* in the Greek means to be in the company, associate with, and even have intercourse; it means to communicate.

These environments are both hazardous to your spiritual health and wellbeing and can ultimately be morbid and lethal. Yes, the root of bitterness is a lethal weapon of Satan. Don't allow yourself to be infected; let's uproot and erase the fault lines caused by the root of bitterness.

Remember, we are agents of change; channels of grace whereby water springs forth to revive and refresh. Everyone we come into contact with should taste and see that the Lord is good.

"O taste and see that the Lord is good: blessed is the man that trusteth in him" Psalm 34:8.

Chapter 5

From Bitter to Better

5

From Bitter to Better

"And when they came to Marah, they could not drink of
the waters of Marah, for they were bitter: therefore the name of it
was called Marah." Exodus 15:23

Another lesson I learned in the country is how to enjoy the fruit of the land. My great aunt was born in 1900 and as I can recall, she spoke of a time when stores for them were secondary. They raised livestock and grew vegetables. So, at times when we didn't have money to go to the sweet shops or corner stores, we would pick figs, berries, pears, and something called persimmons.

Persimmons were grown in America and Japan. They were sweet, but had to go through a process. If picked too soon, they would taste very bitter but when allowed to process, the bitter became sweet.

The lesson here is if we allow ourselves to heal, we can ulti-mately become better. You can become better after the heartbreak, divorce, abuse in your place of employment, or even your home amongst family. If you allow God to do it, He can turn it around. When we neglect to do this, we find ourselves masking the wound and attempt to build on a fault line. We often call this *rebound relationships*. These never last because they neglect to treat the hurt and only address the fruit.

So often, two people with deep, past hurts take flight rather than fight, because no one wants to confront their own inner fault lines but rather fault others for what is within. Let's be honest— men have fault lines just as women. Usually, men hide theirs because they have been taught to never show weakness but remember, you cannot conquer what you refuse to confront.

"You will never conquer what you refuse to confront."

Let us take a moment and see how dangerous a hurting individual can be to those closest to them.

Chapter 6

Crouching Tiger, and Hidden Dragon

6

Crouching Tiger, and Hidden Dragon

"And the Lord said unto Cain, Why art thou wroth? And why is thy countenance fallen? If thou doeth well, shalt thou not be accepted? And if thou doeth not well, sin lieth at the door. And unto thee shall be his desire, and thou must rule over him." Genesis 4:7

One of the first capital crimes ever committed can be attributed to a fault line. Let's visit the crime scene. Adam and Eve's sons Cain and Abel had what was unique for the time, but quite common today. They both worshiped God with an offering. Cain was a farmer and Abel was a shepherd. Abel's offering was distinctly different because he offered the choice, or best, of his flock. Cain just brought an offering. God favored Abel's offering but not Cain's. Abel valued the Father in such a way, he gave Him the firstling of his flock. But rather than change his offering, something sprung up in Cain that got God's attention.

Notice that it wasn't Cain's words, but his attitude and demeanor that God acknowledged. He was angry, and he had what I would say was an angry, bitter facial expression. God warned him because he was preparing to commit premeditated murder. Yes, Cain's anger was about to be taken out on his brother because he was blessed, accepted, and favored by God the Father.

What I like about this text is that God exposed the fault line in Cain and warned of the danger of ignoring and not repenting of this toxic root. Listen to what He says that this door of offense is like—*a door can allow sin like a crouching tiger lieth at the door.* "Door" as him being positioned to pounce when it is open. But also that if he opened the door, or gave him access, he would control you instead of you mastering him. But yet God says to him that he can change and be accepted if he did what was right. Cain elected to do the opposite and was exiled and marked.

How often, rather than change, do we point the finger at others? We allow the bait of Satan to seduce us to open a door and invite the hidden dragon and crouching tiger in to manipulate us into committing egregious crimes against those close to us. The anger festered, the jealousy and bitterness grew, until murder was the case.

We may not physically murder but our words can be lethal. Our words can slander, cripple, and destroy the name of those we love due to our faulty root system, due our bitterness and refusal to allow the Word of God to be our guide in our quest for peace. Cain chose bitterness rather than becoming better by uprooting and erasing the fault line to destiny.

These fault lines are usually not noticed and those who have those issues are labeled less than sane, to say the least. Their actions don't initially have nefarious motives but the more they fester, the more toxic and lethal their actions become. Cain and Abel gave us a glimpse into even the closest relationship being siblings. We would never believe that such anger and bitterness would be expressed from one to the other. But also we understand that hidden in plain sight was the signs though very little is known of Cain. We can assume due from the statement of God that there was much more than meets the eye.

"Having therefore these promises, dearly beloved, let us cleanse ourselves from all filthiness of the flesh and spirit, perfecting holiness in the fear of God" 2 Corinthians 7:1.

This scripture not only exposes the filth that can contaminate both flesh and spirit, but it also reveals that it begins from within. The New International Version of the scripture says *to purify ourselves of everything that contaminates the body and spirit*. It gives hope to the reader that you can transition from bitterness to being a better person. Let us look at another brother that was exposed when he was given the love test.

"And he called one of the servants, and asked what these things meant. And he said unto him, thy brother is come; and thy father hath killed the fatted calf, because he hath received him safe and sound. And he was angry and would not go in: therefore came his father out to him" Luke 15:26-28.

Here, we have another situation in which faulty lines are exposed. The popular story of the Prodigal Son often highlights the juvenile errors of a young son. His hardships, loss, and restoration. It also highlights the grace and love of a father. But Jesus saw fit to give insight into the elder brother's response to the return of his younger brother.

At a time when the family should have been rejoicing at the return of the lost son, we see another spirit dominating the elder brother. To the extent that he reacted the total opposite of what was right. If there ever was a time that would justify a family celebration, this was it. But instead of celebrating his anger, jealousy manifested to the point where he refused to enter. He didn't even ask concerning the wellbeing of his younger brother. But instead, I can imagine him sitting there pouting like a child and not conducting himself as a man.

Listen to his justification for his actions:

"And he answered and said unto his father, Lo these many years do I serve thee, neither transgressed I at any time thy commandment; and yet thou never gavest me kid, that I may

make merry with my friends: But as soon as this thy son was come, which devoured thy living with harlots, thou hast killed for him the fatted calf" Luke 15:29.

His explanation actually attacked the son and reminded the father of his indiscretions. He never said his brother, but rather he said, *thy son.* I can hear the arrogance, disrespect, and bitterness in his tone when he said *thy son.* He listed all that he did while at the same time exalting himself as being flawless, loyal, and faithful. Then, at the same time, he questioned the father's decision making and consciousness of who he was and what he sacrificed throughout the year. He even placed blame on the killing of the fatted calf, which was customary for a celebration. The calf, riotous living, prostitutes, and the waste of the money the father gave him was an attempt to justify his nasty, toxic spirit. But as a father always does, he reminded him of his position and inheritance.

How often in our families, homes, communities, and churches is the fruit judged, but the root is not dealt with? If we remove the source, which is the root, we can erase the fault line and have great success.

In his book, *Feeling Good: The New Mood of Therapy Cognitive Behavior[i]*, therapist David Burns identifies several cognitive distortions and patterns of thinking that are false and the source of distress in many. One of them is *personalization* in which we accept responsibility rather than assigning blame or fault to someone or something for our condition.

A great example of taking ownership and experiencing love and forgiveness can be seen in King David when confronted about his transgression. He quickly acknowledged his faults and repented, thus experiencing grace and forgiveness.

"And David said unto Nathan, I have sinned against the LORD. And Nathan said unto David, The LORD also hath put away thy sin; thou shalt not die" 2 Samuel 12:13.

This is evident in the account of the Prodigal Son and his elder brother. We refuse to embrace the responsibility that is necessary for change. This must be done before healing can occur. There is a celebration that awaits us if only we can identify and deal with the core faulty root symptom that continues to hinder and stifle our growth. An opportunity to enter into a place of joyous celebration.

Chapter 7

Marah and Elim, the Path to Promise

7

Marah and Elim, the Path to Promise

"And they removed from Marah, and came unto Elim: and in Elim were twelve fountains of wa-
ter, and threescore and ten palm trees; and they pitched there."
Numbers 33:9

Sometimes, in order to truly be free and experience the Fruit of the Spirit, we must recognize that we will pass through uncomfortable seasons of resistance, betrayal, affliction, and lies. This does not mean that you are not on the right path but rather you are on course for something greater.

A wonderful example of this is found in the Book of Exodus whereby the great prophet and leader Moses led the people from Egypt through the Red Sea and set their sights on the Promised Land. Miriam and Moses sang on the sandy beaches of the Red Sea a song of victory after experiencing the glorious power of

God's deliverance. Now, three days into the journey, they are thirsty and discontented.

*"So Moses brought Israel from the Red Sea, and they went into the wilderness of Shur; and they went three days in the wilderness, and found no water. And when they came to **Marah**, they could not drink the waters of Marah, for they were bitter: therefore the name of it was called Marah. And the people murmured against Moses, saying, saying what shall we drink"* Exodus 15:22-24.

Marah is believed to have possessed a well in the desert eight feet wide and two feet deep. Scholars believed that it contained sulfate of lime, magnesia, soda, potash, chloride of sodium, silicic acid, and other chemicals that made it unfit for drinking. Can you imagine their frustration when thirsty and finally after a three day journey, they discover a well with water that is brackish. As is such with many people we encounter; they look the part, but the well-spring has been contaminated so that we cannot drink of their water and taste and see that the Lord is good.

The waters of *Marah* symbolized the spiritual and mental state of many people. Yes, they were liberated from Pharaoh but yet there was a root that poisoned the waters. The potential to be a refreshment. A well-spring of hope in a desert place for the thirsty soul is the potential for the Church of Jesus Christ but yet we have become a place of bitterness. But again, I say, there is hope!

Listen to their response. They cried out of desperation to Moses since he was the leader of this recently liberated nation in the wilderness. Rather than petitioning God, they focused on Moses! Yet another test in which we have double exposure to the fault lines of people.

"And he cried to the Lord and the Lord showed him a tree, which when he had cast it into the waters, the waters were made sweet: there he made of them a statute and ordinance, and there he proved them" Exodus 15:25.

How wonderful and marvelous it is that our God has provided for us in every state. As wonderful as finding the well is, it is just as wonderful that God revealed to Moses after prayer the antidote for the bitter and brackish waters. I'm not sure how long it took for the tree to grow nor how long the waters were bitter, but I know that the tree was sufficient to make the bitter waters sweet. Such it is with us; we endure much counsel, many sermons, even the advice of friends and family. But yet the true antidote for our bitter waters is a tree that has grown from the root and offspring of David.

"I Jesus have sent mine angel to testify unto you these things in the churches. I am the root and the offspring of David, and the bright and morning star" Revelation 22:16.

It is only when you apply that beautiful cross. The image of grace to our bitter waters can that which was unsuitable to drink become refreshing. It is there at *Marah* that our Lord reveals Himself to be Jehovah Rophi! The Lord that healeth thee (vs. 26).

But that is not the end of the account. The Bible shares with us that the path they took was through Marah and the next station was a place called *Elim*.

"And they came to Elim, where were twelve wells of water, and three score and ten (seventy) palm trees" Exodus 15:27.

Elim means *place of strong trees and trees of God*. They were steps away from an oasis in the desert, from Marah to Elim. A well for every tribe and shade from the heat. God will take you from bitterness to a better life. He provides and heals at Marah and satisfies our mouths with good things at Elim where we come under the Shadow of His wings.

It is evident that within the congregation in the wilderness were fault lines that were exposed when they were under stress.

Tricks are for Kids!
Don't Play the Blame Game

8

Tricks are for Kids!
Don't Play the Blame Game

"Whereas angels, which are greater in power and might, bring not railing accusation against them before the Lord."
2 Peter 2:11

Blame (*mamaomai*, Greek) means to "find fault." In Sociology, individual blame is **the tendency of a group or society to hold the individual responsible for his or her situation**, whereas system blame is *the tendency to focus on social factors that contribute to one's fate.*

It is common and easy for a person when they have been caught in an uncomfortable situation, one where there are consequences, to immediately defer responsibility to someone, or something, besides self. We live in a society where everyone is a victim of someone else. Politicians, employers and employees, husbands and wives, races, and even religions. No one seems to convert from the victim to the victor's mentality. We cannot ascend to the levels of greatness God designed us to be if we continue to cast off responsibility on others. Sure, others can contribute to your fall, but our God has given you the power to rise again. In the blame game, only Satan wins. What we do when we participate is we relinquish power for destiny fulfillment to others. And thus, our success is dependent upon their grace.

Listen to these quotes from those who play the victim. It's not my fault! I was abused as a child. I wasn't given opportunity. I have too much melanin in my skin; therefore, I'm not accepted. He abandoned me with these children. I'm sure you have heard these statements or even quoted them yourself. Doesn't it sound like the kid that said the dog ate my homework? Now, I don't make light of any of those situations and they are factual in many cases. But our past can prevent our future when we allow it to be a prison of pain and regret. You can get back up again. You can live beyond the hurt. You can build again on solid ground.

Tricks are for Kids

"And he said, Who told thee that thou wast naked? Hast thou eaten of the tree, whereof I commanded thee that thou shouldest not eat? And the man said, The woman whom thou gavest to be with me, she gave me of the tree, and I did eat. And the LORD God said unto the woman, What is this that thou hast done? And the woman said, The serpent beguiled me, and I did eat" Genesis 3:11-13.

Doesn't this sound familiar? They both confessed to the transgression but yet they shifted the blame. Adam blamed God's action in making provision for his companionship and caused him to sin. He actually blamed God and his wife. His wife blamed the snake. As one writer said, "Adam blamed Eve, Eve blamed the snake, and the snake didn't have a leg to stand on."

In all of the blame going on in Scripture, God yet judged them all. Blame wasn't justified by God; therefore, humanity was judged. But praise be unto God for the second Adam, Jesus Christ our Lord, that when we confess, He delivers us from the consequences of fallen man's actions.

Confession is a key component of God's formula for inner healing. Even while visiting your physician, transparency is key to identifying and addressing the root cause of a thing. Finding the fault line and pointing it out is the beginning of healing and victory. Both the violator and the offended must take personal responsibility in order to experience true victory in that area. Thus, introspection is critical. Introspection provides an opportunity to change and strengthen the weakness within us that is justified by blaming others and deferring fault.

"Introspection without application of self-knowledge and awareness to bring about positive change is wasted opportunity."

Introspection gives revelation of inner faults but application is the disciple to do what is necessary to experience change and to have a healthy relationship on every front.

Yes, I understand that self-examination is painful because being brutally honest requires us to embrace the fact that we are flawed, and have weaknesses and shortcomings. But our faults can be strengthened when we submit to God. He gives us power to resist the devil and he flees from our presence.

"Introspection will lead to retrospection, which gives us protection for sustained progression."

Where Did You Lose It?

"Let us go, we pray thee, unto Jordan, and take thence every man a beam, and let us make us a place there, where we may dwell. And he answered, Go ye. And one said, Be content, I pray thee, and go with thy servants. And he answered, I will go. So he went with them. And when they came to Jordan, they cut down wood. But as one was felling a beam, the axe head fell into the water: and he cried, and said, Alas, master! for it was borrowed. And the man of God said, Where fell it? And he shewed him the place. And he cut down a stick, and cast it in thither; and the iron did swim. Therefore said he, Take it up to thee. And he put out his hand, and took it" 2 Kings 6:2-7.

This scripture gives us a wonderful example of how important it is for us to identify not only the problem, but also the timing that triggered the experience. It tells the account of someone who began to build along with his brethren and proceeded to build in order to satisfy the need for a more suitable meeting place. But as they were building, one of them experienced a loss that would not only affect him fulfilling his portion of the responsibility. It would be costly financially, and possibly putting a strain on his relationship with the person who lent him the axe. Certainly, you would expect him to replace what was borrowed and lost. But consider that he did not have an axe of his own so possibly, he could not afford one. Imagine the stress, the emotional turmoil that he was experiencing. How do I even tell my friend from whom I borrowed the axe from what has happened? Maybe, I can say that the axe head wasn't connected securely, so that he will see it's not my fault!

But rather, he approached his leader. He approached and sought counsel with a man of God. And the counsel that he provided was amazing and relevant even today. He asked the question, "Where did it fall?" Or "Where did you lose it?" His progress was impeded but wisdom was what he needed. The counsel that Elisha gave him is common whenever therapy is required. Let us identify when, where, and what are the triggers. It was only after he confessed where he lost it that the Prophet was able to assist him in retrieving it. Thus, eliminating the beginning of a costly and uncomfortable relationship. As well as impeding progress and vision fulfillment.

How often do we overlook life's triggers? We refuse to reflect on the circumstances and situations that contribute to loss; therefore, we continue to repeat the same class only to fail.

"Those who do not learn from the past are doomed to repeat it." — **George Santayana**

Selective ignorance, or sometimes called *tactical ignoring*, will never heal past hurts, but rather weaponize your past and guarantee doom and destruction is your forecast.

"My people are destroyed for lack of knowledge: because thou hast rejected knowledge, I will also reject thee, that thou shalt be no priest to me: seeing thou hast forgotten the law of thy God, I will also forget thy children" Hosea 4:6.

The aggressor, or offender, will never be comfortable with the painful truth regarding their actions. So, they will work tirelessly to justify and erase the memory of the past. And as we have stated, they are doomed to repeat it. Satan wins when we don't acknowledge and learn from our mistakes. Behavior change is never desired, or applied, when this approach becomes habitual.

So, rather than going on a fault finding expedition, exploring the fault of others, let's take personal responsibility and allow God to heal us first. Hurting people can be dangerous and toxic to themselves and to others. We can be a danger to ourselves and those closest to us. We should desire to be a spring of refreshing waters, rather than a dead sea of unfiltered saltwater.

> "Blame judges a situation
> And assigns the cause of the hurt
> To be someone else's fault."
> "If you don't heal
> From what hurt you
> You will bleed on the people
> Who never cut you."
> — **Unknown**

Many may believe it is easy to say that we shouldn't play the blame game, because it seems if you allow them to get away with their offense that they will feel as if they are justified in their actions. Consider the cost of always laying blame at the feet of others, even when it is justified. It can stifle your growth, influence future relationships, and torment you to the point that you abandon the peace that has been ordained of God for you to enjoy. Remember that peace is a Fruit of the Spirit, but worry and stress is a fruit of the root of bitterness.

In life and ministry, I have counseled many people that have had valid reasons for finding legitimate fault with the actions of others, whether it is a friend, associate, or even family member that has abused their relationship and caused great hurt. For example, the dishonesty of a friend, the neglect or even abuse of a spouse, or the lack of support and affection of a parent. When considering our plight in life, we blame others for our mental, physical, sexual, and socioeconomic conditions. This perception of hurt and who's to blame, if not dealt with correctly, can become a cage. This cage of time traps many and each session, they retract back to what, or who, hurt them with no progress in sight.

I call this the *Groundhog Day Experience*. In 1993, a movie directed by Harold Ramsi and starring Bill Murray hit the screens and was almost an instant hit. It tracked the life of Phil Conners, played by Murray, being trapped to every day repeat the same thing. To many, this was a comedy but to me, it was a horror story. Conners had to repeat the same thing over and over again. He was in a perpetual time loop. An emotional treadmill. A cycle of frustration. The only thing that could deliver him from this terror was that he had to discover the error of his ways and change. When this was performed, he was allowed to move on to the next day.

Doesn't this sound familiar? How often through blame do we continue to reenact the same hurtful experience? Doing so traps us in our own *personal groundhog day*. We can change geographically, grow into adults, divorce and remarry, and even move our membership to other churches. But yet if inner healing doesn't take place, we will carry with us a fault line that under stress, will produce the same earthquake as before. It's time to break the cycle of hurt and pain. It's time to wake up from the nightmare of constant disappointment by choosing to be a victor rather than a victim. They hurt you, but now what? They lied about you, but you know the truth. They abused you and betrayed you, but how will you respond? In some cases years, months, and decades have passed and yet you are trapped in a *groundhog day* when the Lord has set before you the opportunity for life.

"Bitterness is unmitigated anger that has been allow to seed, germinate, and take root in the heart."

"Be not hasty in thy spirit to be angry: for anger resteth in the bosom of fools" Ecclesiastes 7:9.

Remember to be angry, but don't allow the anger to burn within your heart to the point that you fall short of the glory of God and sin. Winning requires discipline, effort, and a winning attitude. Winners have a certain mentality that takes the same anger that causes most to sin and uses it to be the fuel in the vehicle that drives you to the finish line of victory.

The late great 5 time NBA champion Kobe Bryant when speaking concerning hurt and pain said:

"Pain doesn't tell you when you ought to stop. Pain is the little voice in your head that tries to hold you back because it knows if you continue you will change. Don't let it stop you from being who you can be. Exhaustion tells you when you ought to stop. You only reach your limit when you can go no further." — **Kobe Bean Bryant**

What Lies Beneath

I live in a part of the country that is known for very intense storms—storms that can cause catastrophic damages. It is evident that every region has its potential problems. Earthquakes and fires on the West Coast, tornadoes in the Midwest, snowstorms and blizzards to the North, and yes, hurricanes in the South. Living in the South, you must be prepared for storms which can occur unexpectedly during what is known as *hurricane season*. This is usually from June 1st to November 30th. It is important to have your basic necessities during that time but what is just as important is having a dwelling suitable to sustain intense winds and even flood waters. Homes are generally built with storm windows, storm doors, and strong material to endure inclement weather. But as with all things, the most important aspect of the structure is rarely seen. Yes, you guessed it, the foundation!

"Therefore whosoever heareth these sayings of mine, and doeth them, I will liken him unto a wise man, which built his house upon a rock: And the rain descended, and the floods came, and the winds blew, and beat upon that house; and it fell not: for it was founded upon a rock. And every one that heareth these sayings of mine, and doeth them not, shall be likened unto a foolish man, which built his house upon the sand: And the rain descended, and the floods came, and the winds blew, and beat

upon that house; and it fell: and great was the fall of it" Luke 6:46-49.

It may appear that there are two characters in this scripture, one wise and one foolish. But there are actually three that we can refer to. The third, who should be first, is the Rock:

"Trust in the LORD always, for the LORD God is the eternal Rock" Isaiah 26:4, NLV.

Our text gives such wonderful examples of the distinct differences that occur during the building process. Our Lord Himself gives an analysis that we should take heed to. These individuals set a charter to build a home. The homes appeared to be complete but as with any structure, there are certain tests that must take place in order to be considered qualified for occupancy. Jesus identifies the difference in the two. One took the time to invest in the foundation, making sure there was depth and firmness in which to lay the foundation. The other took the route of least resistance and built on a carnal, corrupt foundation of earth alone. They both experienced storms but the results were not the same.

"That ye may be the children of your Father which is in heaven: for he maketh his sun to rise on the evil and on the good, and sendeth rain on the just and on the unjust" Matthew 5:45.

We should note that storms are inevitable in life, whether natural or spiritual. These storms will test the fabric and makeup of your building. But it is obedience to the Word of God and the application that will ultimately give you staying power. Notice, the foundation is rarely seen but its results are clearly noticed. Building your house, marriage, relationship with your kids, career, and even your ministry on faulty soil will never last. The investment, the time, and the effort that it takes to dig beneath the surface to lay a strong and firm foundation will pay everlasting benefits.

I implore you to commit to getting the help you need through the Word of God in order to build an enduring example of strength and longevity for all to see. Founded not only in knowledge of His Word, but also in the application of the same.

As the songwriter says, "On Christ the Solid Rock I stand—all other ground is sinking sand."

It's Time to Come Clean!
Erasing Dangerous Fault Lines

9

It's Time to Come Clean!
Erasing Dangerous Fault Lines

"Examine me, O Lord, and prove me; try my reins and my heart."
Psalm 26:2

Just the Tip of the Iceberg

In order to walk in victory as a healed and whole Believer, we have to learn to perform self-examination first. What are the reasons for my behavior? Because the visible reaction to a crisis, even the tremors of life, are only the tip of the iceberg. Thus, we refer to a clinical theory known as the *iceberg theory*.

The iceberg theory is a frequently cited model of behavior which states that a person's behavior can only be properly understood in the context of the factors that caused it. What a person does is "the tip of the iceberg"—what we don't see are the emotional, social, cultural, and other factors that lie beneath the surface and cause that behavior.

The premise of this theory acknowledges that similar to an iceberg, our lives have different vantage points. The obvious which is seen in behavior and our actions. But there is still more than what meets the eye. Just like an iceberg, we only see the tip which is considered to measure only 10% of the mass. The other 90% is beneath the waters and requires more depth in order to know its range. Ignoring the total mass can be catastrophic and cause titanic-like destruction.

"And the counsel of Ahithophel, which he counselled in those days, was as if a man had inquired at the oracle of God: so was all the counsel of Ahithophel both with David and with Absalom" 2 Samuel 16:23.

"Moreover Ahithophel said unto Absalom, Let me now choose out twelve thousand men, and I will arise and pursue after David this night: And I will come upon him while he is weary and weak handed, and will make him afraid: and all the people that are with him shall flee; and I will smite the king only: And I will bring back all the people unto thee: the man whom thou seekest is as if all returned: so all the people shall be in peace. And the saying pleased Absalom well, and all the elders of Israel" 2 Samuel 17:1-4.

There are very few credible prophets in the Bible possessing the testimony of Ahithophel. He was known for his accuracy when giving counsel. He was a trusted cabinet member of King David, known as King David's chief counsel. Of course, in order to be such an important and vital voice to the King and a part of his inner circle, required not only skill, but trust. These words were evident. In verse 23, when it said that he had this testimony, he spoke as he was providing words that appeared to come directly from the mouth of God. Now, we see him conspiring with David's enemy Absalom, his son, concerning assassinating the King. Not only so, but he desired to perform the assassination himself.

What would cause such a drastic change in attitude to the point where bitterness and hatred would arise in someone once so loyal? Further examination of the Word of God reveals that Ahithophel was the grandfather of Bathsheba (2 Samuel 23:34), and it is possible he was not pleased with the actions of the King regarding his granddaughter and his grandson in law. We could only imagine the hurt, anger, and bitterness that festered unhindered in the heart of this great prophet. He desired to kill the kin with his own hands. This drove him to do the unthinkable when his counsel was not heeded.

"And when Ahithophel saw that his counsel was not followed, he saddled his ass, and arose, and gat him home to his house, to his city, and put his household in order, and hanged himself, and died, and was buried in the sepulchre of his father" 2 Samuel 17:23.

What a tragic end to a once illustrious ministry. The tragedy was just the tip of the iceberg. The culture, climate, and actions of others contributed to his demise. But yet the final decision still resided within himself. It's dangerous to allow unmitigated anger to rest in your bosom. The results can cost you your life. We have a blessed opportunity to address and overcome these unsavory experiences. God has given us the power to be victors and no longer victims. We all have valid reasons to be angry due to the many offenses of people who never knew our true value. But the victory is in the choice that we have in Christ to seize the liberty that He offers and overcome our past.

Drop Your Rocks

"And the scribes and Pharisees brought unto him a woman taken in adultery; and when they had set her in the midst, They say unto him, Master, this woman was taken in adultery, in the very act. Now Moses in the law commanded us, that such should be stoned: but what sayest thou? This they said, tempting him, that they might have to accuse him. But Jesus stooped down, and with his finger wrote on the ground, as though he heard them not. So when they continued asking him, he lifted up himself, and said unto them, He that is without sin among you, let him first cast a stone at her. And again he stooped down, and wrote on the ground. And they which heard it, being convicted by their own conscience, went out one by one, beginning at the eldest, even unto the last: and Jesus was left alone, and the woman standing in the midst. When Jesus had lifted up himself, and saw none but the woman, he said unto her, Woman, where are those thine accusers? hath no man condemned thee? She said, No

man, Lord. And Jesus said unto her, Neither do I condemn thee: go, and sin no more" John 8:3-10.

I've learned not to participate in the selfish games that people play when it comes to the fall of others. Knowing that we must be aware that we are one misstep away from a fall ourselves. Being critical is both foolish and juvenile. Growth desires to help the hurting and learn from our mistakes. Focus and discipline are essential to fulfill destiny and live a healthy Christian life. Our treatment of others is a reflection of our maturity and consciousness of the grace gifted us by our Lord that covers our sins. When we ignore our faults but magnify the faults of others, we reject the golden rule found in Mark 12:31, which tells us to love our neighbors as ourselves.

Jesus once again uses life encounters to give spiritual revelation to His followers and even His haters. A situation that we have often heard about was brought to Him. But they had impure motives instigated by those who assumed the position of authority and thus challenged His knowledge of the law, so that they may, as the scripture reveals, *have an accusation against Him.* But the Master, as always, knows the motives and intents of the heart. They saw Him only as a prophet, but not the very expression of grace.

This woman's sins and faults were on public display. Can you imagine possibly being torn from the bed in the act of adultery, and now brought naked, figuratively, before the Lord?

Can you imagine the embarrassment that comes with all your business being on public display? Standing there clutching the few pieces of your garment that you were allowed to bring with you as they dragged you away. Not so with the chauvinistic male attitude because there is no record that her male transgressor was brought before our Lord. But yet she said not a word. Her faults were evident and warranted judgment, but Jesus in such a masterful display of grace kneeled to the ground and began to write on the ground.

One could only imagine what He wrote on the ground giving them time to evaluate their claims and challenge Him as it related to His knowledge and fulfillment of the Law. But as grace always does, it rose and spoke for this broken woman saying, "He that is without sin among you, let him cast a stone at her." Then, He proceeded to write again. These words pierced the heart of all her accusers and required them to perform a self-examination before there could be a judgment and punishment. They had to come face to face with their own faults before they could judge hers. And as the Bible declares, they were convicted and went their way beginning with the eldest to the last.

Our Lord presented them with a mirror when they came to Him with a rock. Rather than punish her, He allowed them to see the insufficiencies within themselves. How inadequate they were to assume the role of Judge and Jury in their conspiracy attempt to indict our Lord. It should be noted that the woman was not the target, but our Lord. But this experience resulted in a broken woman being blessed. The Bible said He rose and they all were gone. They had to drop their rocks. Jesus inquired of her something He already knew. *"Where are thou accusers?"* He being the only faultless person before her having the power and right to stone her, chose to extend grace and command her to sin no more.

Let us consider our own shortcomings as we commune with others daily. Let us remember the words of our Lord. Let us remain conscious of the grace that has been extended to us. Grace that erases our faults and gives us a fresh start. As one writer said:

"People living in glass houses should never throw stones."

Listen to the cry of David to God when appealing for help with known and unknown faults in Psalm 139:23, 24:

"Search me, O God, and know my heart: try me, and know my thoughts: And see if there be any wicked way in me, and lead me in the way everlasting."

How wonderful to hear words that proceeded from the lips of a man who is described by God as a man after His own heart, desiring help with his inadequacies and idiosyncrasies. I can imagine him stretching out his hands in total surrender asking God for help. Knowing that his actions and behavior were not always in truth, he directs his prayers to his Creator. And thereby gives Him permission to examine him thoroughly. Now, I understand that the examination is only the beginning but as verse 24 says, *"He will lead us in the way that we should go."* But yet we must follow His instructions to get the desired results. Knowledge of faults is good but the power to administer the necessary actions, as prescribed by God through His Word, requires the help of the Holy Spirit.

How did David confront his faults after being exposed in diabolical behavior towards Uriah and Bathsheba? Initially, he attempted to cover it up but as always, we cannot hide from God. We will never overcome, but rather be overcome with guilt, if we don't surrender to the only help we have and that is the Father. Listen to David's words when confronted by Nathan the prophet:

"To the chief Musician, A Psalm of David, when Nathan the prophet came unto him, after he had gone in to Bathsheba. Have mercy upon me, O God, according to thy lovingkindness: according unto the multitude of thy tender mercies blot out my transgressions. Wash me thoroughly from mine iniquity, and cleanse me from my sin" Psalm 51:1, 2.

A perfect example of the difference between King Saul and King David is that David chose not to make excuses, but rather repent and ask for help from the Father.

Chapter 10

The Vault of Fault

10

The Vault of Fault

"As I walked out the door toward the gate that would lead to my freedom, I knew if I didn't leave my bitterness and hatred behind, I'd still be in prison." — **Nelson Mandela**

These words from the first elected in a fully represented democratic election, President of South Africa, and first black head of state in that country recount and testify of the moment he departed from the Victor Verster prison in Cape Town, South Africa. Being incarcerated for twenty-seven years for fighting for justice and indicted for a conspiracy to overthrow the government, he recognised that there was something he had to do that was necessary to truly be free. And that was to leave bitterness and hatred behind.

"Let all bitterness, and wrath, and anger, and clamour, and evil speaking, be put away from you, with all malice" Ephesians 4:31.

We can only imagine the anguish, pain, and frustration he experienced being separated from family and friends. Deplorable conditions. Basic liberties lost. But yet the resolve to realize that in order to truly be free, he had to release some things and some people.

We should learn from his example. True forgiveness releases the offended, not just the offender. Forgiveness is a choice! This choice is a gift from God; it should be appreciated and valued because it empowers the offended. Remember that when we choose not to forgive, we relinquish that power and surrender to the actions of the offender. The end results are lethal.

"He who is devoid of the power to forgive is devoid of the power to love." — **Martin Luther King, Jr.**

Prisons of old had chains, bars, and guards! I counsel people all the time that live in a prison with invisible bars, chained to the pain of the past and guarded by fear and terror that if they would ever forgive, they become vulnerable for future hurt. Therefore, they live holding the keys to be free but refuse to use them because they would also release the person that has caused them harm. Selfishness and pride justifies their actions and instead of hurting the person that hurt them, they consistently inflict pain by revisiting the hurt from the past. The wounds never heal because they are never addressed and treated.

A prime example of this is given in the life of Job. It is debatable how long he suffered afflictions through the attacks of the enemy, but one thing is clear; he possessed the keys to his liberty and restoration. Notice, when he was released from his captivity what took place in his life.

"And the LORD turned the captivity of Job, when he prayed for his friends: also the LORD gave Job twice as much as he had before" Job 42:10.

I must say it was worth it: the friends that misjudged him, accused him, and scolded him, the wife that provoked him, and the devil that attacked him. But yet he prayed for his friends never changing their status as friends due to fault, and God released him and his rewards. He erased the fault lines. He didn't play the blame game. He chose love and was released of his affliction and rewarded for his faithfulness.

"Genuine prayer comes from a pure heart that has not been contaminated by hatred and fueled by the nectar from the root of bitterness."

"If I regard iniquity in my heart, the Lord will not hear me" Psalm 66:18.

"Just remember, forgiveness is a way of setting yourself free of the bondage placed on you by others." — **Tracie Peterson**

Those that choose to judge others for their conditions and place them at fault for their current position become prisoners to an offense and thus chain themselves to the past, giving the key to their deliverance to the offender who may never choose to set you free. Therefore, we must choose to be free by choosing to forgive, recognizing that there is more to their behavior than meets the eye. This will help you to maintain a position of liberty, and not bondage, after you have been liberated by the Savior in every aspect of your life.

Remember, freedom is a choice. Emotional, cognitive, and even spiritual freedom is a choice offered to us by the Father and acquired and maintained by the Son. The benefits of this choice to be free are far reaching. Your behavior with oneself, as well as your treatment of others, is a result of your liberty. I know you say easier said than done but I can assure you that it is possible, because I myself had to learn how to embrace each experience as one of learning. Not merely of learning the traits and behaviors of others, but through every experience, I learned what was within me rather good or bad.

"To grow yourself you must know yourself." —**John Maxwell**

Chapter 11

Debt Free

11

Debt Free

"Therefore, brethren, we are debtors, not to the flesh, to live after the flesh." Romans 8:12

Weakness or Wickedness

I grew up during a time in which respect for your elders was demanded and not suggested. A time in which you did not participate in the conversations of elders but rather you removed yourself even from the company of what we called *grown up conversations*. The results of your rebellion to the, at times, unspoken rules were serious to say the least. A time when the wrath, or consequences, of bad behavior were severe and could potentially last for days. Yes, our elders believed in Proverb 13:24.

"He who spares his rod hates his son, But he who loves him disciplines him promptly."

And normally, this was carried out by the father-figure in the home. Now, I will admit sometimes these actions were not performed with the love and grace that you would expect. But a key to my victory was understanding the person and purpose behind the pain, and how to overcome the offense.

I don't believe that anyone reading this book likes debt. Debt is demanding and weighty to say the least. Right now, if someone approached you and said they were paying off all your debts, you would erupt in praise. Because debt is bondage. Listen to what the wise man says about debt:

"The rich ruleth over the poor, and the borrower is servant to the lender" Proverb 22:7.

Another translation exchanges the word servant for *slave*. Thus, giving a more vivid example of the bondages of debt. But this does not only refer to tangible wealth and debt. If you will allow me to provoke some thought through the scripture, you will see that being offended and holding onto offense is similar to holding onto death.

"And forgive us our debts, as we forgive our debtors" Matthew 6:12.

Our Lord, in the model, prays something that is very profound and challenging at the same time. He refers to unforgiveness as debts owed, and a key to us getting our debt relief is our conduct when handling someone else's offense. This is critical, but possible, when you deal with your internal issues, or fault lines. Moving on from the residue of past hurt and experiencing inner healing and victory.

Now, ask yourself the question: Did the Father forgive me for my transgressions? If the answer is yes, then the correct response for that type of grace is through passing it on to others. Again, remember that unforgiveness is like holding someone's debt. And like debt, you are chained to them until they pay what you deem sufficient.

Jesus says that in life, it is guaranteed that you will be on one side or the other of offense. Let us look at His prayer in the Book of John.

"Then said he unto the disciples, It is impossible but that offences will come: but woe unto him, through whom they come!" John 17:1.

He guarantees here that offenses will be a part of life. Also, that you do not want to be the offender. But if this is going to be a common occurrence, I would like to know how to overcome these experiences. First, you must understand that an offense is a trap. Every trap's success depends upon the bait and deception of the perpetrator. Vine's Expository Dictionary describes an offense (*skandalon*) as the part of a trap where the bait is set. So, if that is correct, then we must assume that Satan can only trap us when we fall for that which seduces us. Yes, he appeals to our appetite to ultimately entrap us by the things that we enjoy.

"But every man is tempted, when he is drawn away of his own lust, and enticed" James 1:14.

Offenses begin within and not without. I cannot be offended if I check my lust to be the victim.

I want to give you a few clues to conquering offense and living a debt-free life. First, your perception is important. Most of the debts that I held in life were the result of my perception of the transgression. If I judged the action to be nefarious, then I would not only hold onto it, but I would also retaliate. But when I viewed it from a different vantage point, I was able to both forgive and forget. So, with each offense, I asked the question was this wickedness or a weakness? When it is a weakness, my response would be different.

"But I say unto you, Love your enemies, bless them that curse you, do good to them that hate you, and pray for them which despitefully use you, and persecute you;" Matthew 5:44.

From a place of strength, love, and power, you can relieve a person's debt. You can extend grace and love because you see weakness, not wickedness. Then, you will not hold debt but forgive debt, so that you and the offender will live in harmony.

"Then said Jesus, Father, forgive them; for they know not what they do. And they parted his raiment, and cast lots" Luke 23:34.

Even in the midst of the most gruesome capital punishment, our Lord maintained a position of Love. One that covers the transgressions of others. Can you imagine what He endured at the hands of those who also qualified for His grace? He attributed their actions to ignorance. A weakness and not a wickedness. Because He was rooted and grounded in love, He did not blame others, or even fault others, for their actions, but rather asked for their forgiveness. What amazing love is expressed!

How wonderful it is to have such an example of grace and mercy. This should testify to us all the possibilities of *agape*, the unconditional love of God. The possibilities of love when you are firmly anchored in the Love of God. You may say, "But this is Jesus not me." But remember, Christ dwells in your heart by faith (Ephesians 3:17). And since He does, He empowers you and I to do what He does. He's not a squatter just taking up space, but He is there to work within and without. Yes, this is a process. Not on God's end but rather our own. We must yield to Him through acceptance, confession, and repentance, and be Christlike even when we are not at fault.

I have learned this can be accomplished when you know the truth. Because unlike facts that change, truth can stand on its own. It needs no defense nor any mediator. Truth is the ultimate reality, and Jesus is the Truth. The truth about you is not how others view you, but how God sees you—what God says about you. Because if you see things through the lens of anyone and anything but the Creator, then you will be prisoner to the limits and limitations placed upon you by individuals and things that don't really matter. You become voluntary slaves to their opinions. This leads to acceptance of a false reality, which is not true. Just because we make mistakes, doesn't make us a mistake.

Our past doesn't have to determine our future. We have been destined for dominion, blessed for battle, favored in the midst of famine, and called to conquer!

Chapter 12

The Conqueror in You!

12

The Conqueror in You!

"Nay, in all these things we are more than conquerors through him that loved us." Romans 8:37

When we recognize the root cause of the emotional eruptions and earthquakes in our lives, it's easy to be discouraged. But it should be rather encouraging because you now know what you must address before you can have healthy relationships. Yes, knowledge of this helps you identify those triggers that can make you undesirable and unapproachable. Has anyone ever said to you after they had a chance to get to know you that they assumed you were mean because of your demeanor? In some cases, this is a sign of discontent and inner turmoil.

"You will never conquer what you refuse to confront."

I have often counseled couples that began their relationships and marriage with great zeal and promise but somewhere along the way, as they pursued the more perfect union called marriage, they hit a wall. Yes, it has been said that every relationship has at least four stages:

- ❖ Attraction
- ❖ Attachment
- ❖ **Crisis**
- ❖ Commitment

The *crisis stage* is usually the stage when hidden fault lines are exposed. At this time, fight or flight is demanded. We begin to appraise our relationship and the necessary investment to have success. But usually, flight occurs and we shut down to keep the peace. The fault lines produce an earthquake and then an eruption that exposes our weakness.

Like earthquake fault lines, relationship fault lines lie submerged in deep, largely unexpressed feelings of anger, resentment, disappointment, distrust, and disillusionment. Personally, I've seen many relationships in jeopardy, not from constant fighting, but from the conflicts that simmer under the surface—the words left unspoken, the disagreements not discussed. Then, a stressor will bring that fault line to the surface, sometimes with disastrous results.

Yet our God has equipped us with what we need to succeed. There is a conquering Jesus within you. He has declared that *"Nay, in all these things you are more than a conqueror."* Acknowledgment is the beginning, but trusting God to help through prayer and application of the Holy Scripture will produce more than any drug or carnal therapy has and ever will. It is His anointing that makes the difference and guarantees good success.

We should remember that the Bible says that we are more than just a conqueror. To better understand this, we must define this word we use frequently in Christian circles. To *conquer* means to overcome, prevail against, to gain a surpassing victory. Wow, just to be a conquer would be enough but He does not limit His views of us by that word alone. He said we are *more than*. I can imagine as it relates to winning that there is no word in the universal vocabulary that describes who we are in Christ. The fault line of betrayal, abuse, rejection, manipulation, neglect, and heartbreak can and will be overcome not survived; conquered when we trust God for His Word. Truly, there is a balm in Gilead. Healing is available.

I cannot count the times in which I have sat across the desk from people, whether couples or individuals, in a state of extreme distress because they were overwhelmed with emotions as a result of what they believed others had done to them. As always, I allow them to vent and express themselves; but deep down, I am waiting for my opportunity to share with them the truth of God's Word and how they are more than a conqueror. Even now, as I am sitting here considering you and your eternal position, your spiritual state and status. Let me encourage you that your current challenge will change you into who you really are. Champions are challenged, but they always win!

I was recently listening to Coach Brian Kelly, who is the winningest coach in Notre Dame football, talk about his spring practices. He was asked what he wanted to accomplish and his reply was, "I wanted to understand our weaknesses going into the summer, so that I could address them." If we could only take this approach, and not sulk in our weakness, but to strengthen our foundation and erase those faults. Remember that there is power in identifying and confessing your faults. The dangers of selective ignorance can alter your natural flow. One example of this occurred with the Mississippi River.

One of the world's most powerful earthquakes changed the course of the Mississippi River in Missouri and created Reelfoot Lake in Tennessee while shaking parts of Arkansas, Kentucky, Illinois, and Ohio. Tremors rattled Boston, New York, and Washington, D.C. "That disaster happened along the New Madrid Seismic Zone in southeast Missouri in late 1811 and early 1812 when three mammoth quakes occurred over several days," said Brian Houser of Quake Kare in St. Louis[ii]. 'Faults that opened in the earth dammed the Mississippi River, redirecting its channel and creating waterfalls that tossed flatboats and killed their crews,' he said. "Other faults and aftershocks dammed a creek in northwest Tennessee that created Reelfoot Lake."

How amazing is this? Those faults could affect a nation and alter the course of the mighty Mississippi River.[iii] Just as these faults affected the nation and even the economy of the United States, relational fault lines can have far reaching effects that can have a damning effect on others. The healing of these can and will give the liberty we desire to move on and build an amazing life.

"Failure is not final as long as faith is present."

Again, as we discussed earlier, *Groundhog Day Syndrome* is the feeling that you are reliving the same day over and over again. Nothing has changed and you are uncontrollably experiencing the same routine. Each of us, at one time or another, has had this experience. The frustration, the anguish, and the stress caused by this could potentially drive someone insane. But yet many suffer through life reliving the same experiences economically and socially. Having the same failing relationships because we search for without what can only be resolved within.

"And a certain man was there, which had an infirmity thirty and eight years. When Jesus saw him lie, and knew that he had been now a long time in that case, he saith unto him, Wilt thou be made whole? The impotent man answered him, Sir, I have no man, when the water is troubled, to put me into the pool: but while I am coming, another steppeth down before me. Jesus saith unto him, Rise, take up thy bed, and walk. And immediately the

man was made whole, and took up his bed, and walked: and on the same day was the sabbath" John 5:5-9.

I can recall taking public transportation in Honolulu Hawaii in 1992. Once I met a young gentleman that was very nice, but also very talkative, and boy could he talk. He talked so much that I missed my stop and ultimately, I had to take another bus to get to my destination. If only I paid more attention, I would have gotten off and saved time. Often, we miss where we should get off and instead, through frustration, we go off. A great lesson was learned from this experience. My problem was not the distraction, but my lack of attention. Distractions are a choice.

"Ye have compassed this mountain long enough: turn you northward" Deuteronomy 6:3.

After forty years of waiting, wandering, whaling, and watching, the people of God receive a message from God as it relates to their journey. It appears that God Himself is fed up and has had enough of them going in circles. As the old songwriter says, "You've got me going in circles." God not only reveals His feelings concerning the constant cycle, but He also gives instructions concerning the actions that should be taken to break the cycle. This is very empowering but also sobering to know that we possess the power to change, but it should be noted that God will not do it for us.

Similarly, when we ignore the underlying issues of the past and choose not to confront the unbalanced fault lines, we enter into new relationships only to experience the same results. A new relationship never heals the hurt but rather postpones the process and masks the pain. I believe that you have spoken within that you are fed up with failing relationships of every kind and you are ready for something different. This will require that you follow God's words and turn towards Him. He is the only one that can heal you everywhere you hurt and help you *erase the fault lines*.

One of the challenges that prolonged Israel's journey in the wilderness was found in the scripture. It should be noted that the strength of a person is revealed when we are under pressure. The people of God find themselves under pressure in the wilderness and begin to feel *nostalgia*.

"Nostalgia is that longing feeling for the past when things seemed better, easier, and fun."

"And the children of Israel said unto them, Would to God we had died by the hand of the LORD in the land of Egypt, when we sat by the flesh pots, and when we did eat bread to the full; for ye have brought us forth into this wilderness, to kill this whole assembly with hunger" Exodus 16:3.

It's amazing how God demonstrated His deliverance power but yet at the first sign of trouble, His people reclined to a day that appealed to the flesh. This seems incredible when we consider the marvelous acts that were performed by the mighty hand of God only to be received with an attitude of *what have you done for me lately* mindset. We see this coming from the chosen towards the Father who is perfect in all His ways.

How much more would it be one to another? A key to overcoming this disorder is when introspection and correction takes place.

Chapter 13

Don't Block Your Blessing

13

Don't Block Your Blessing

"Not rendering evil for evil, or railing for railing: but contrari-
wise blessing; knowing that ye are thereunto called, that ye should
inherit a blessing." 1 Peter 3:9

What's Ahead is Better Than What's Behind

Have you ever wondered why some people cannot have a lasting, healthy relationship with others? That whenever they meet that special someone, or even a mere friendship, it ultimately dissolves. They live their entire life searching for answers, and though everyone involved in the relationship contributes to the success or failure, they go to one extreme in which they blame the other for everything, or they condemn themselves and feel unworthy of a successful, healthy relationship.

A Person with *Borderline Personality Disorder* (BPD), or faulting disorder, struggles with the future due to the pain of the past. The feeling of brokenness and unworthiness causes them to be unstable, fear abandonment, and become impulsive and promiscuous sexually. We see this within the scripture. Even our Lord had to deal with this in His day. For example:

"And he must needs go through Samaria. Then cometh he to a city of Samaria, which is called Sychar, near to the parcel of ground that Jacob gave to his son Joseph. Now Jacob's well was there. Jesus, therefore, being wearied with his journey, sat thus on the well: and it was about the sixth hour. There cometh a woman of Samaria to draw water: Jesus saith unto her, Give me to drink. (For his disciples were gone away unto the city to buy meat.) Then saith the woman of Samaria unto him, How is it that thou, being a Jew, asketh drink of me, which am a woman of Samaria? for the Jews have no dealings with the Samaritans. Jesus answered and said unto her, If thou knewest the gift of God, and who it is that saith to thee, Give me to drink; thou wouldest have asked of him, and he would have given thee living water. The woman saith unto him, Sir, thou hast nothing to draw with, and the well is deep: from whence then hast thou that living water? Art thou greater than our father Jacob, which gave us the well, and drank thereof himself, and his children, and his cattle? Jesus answered and said unto her, Whosoever drinketh of this water shall thirst again: But whosoever drinketh of the water that I shall give him shall never thirst; but the water that I shall give him shall be in him a well of water springing up into everlasting life.

The woman saith unto him, Sir, give me this water, that I thirst not, neither come hither to draw. Jesus saith unto her, Go, call thy husband, and come hither. The woman answered and said, I have no husband. Jesus said unto her, Thou hast well said, I have no husband: For thou hast had five husbands; and he whom thou now hast is not thy husband: in that saidst thou truly. The woman saith unto him, Sir, I perceive that thou art a prophet" John 4:4-19.

Our Lord had a very hectic and intense itinerary during His three and a half year ministry before Calvary. But being led by the Spirit, He instructed His disciples that he NEEDED to make a necessary pit stop in Samaria. Again, need expresses necessity and obligation. And as noted, He not only went to Samaria, but he specifically targeted the local watering hole, or Well of Jacob. Now, it is evident that no one was there to serve Him but yet He was on a mission. One should note that Jacob met Rachel at a well. It could be assumed that the well was a meeting place and if she knew the history as she did of Jacob and Rachel, she would consider it as a place to entertain strangers.

Moses met Zipporah, Abraham's servant met Rebekah, and Even King Saul met young women at a well. Before her was the answer to all of her needs but yet she was not recognized due to her layers of hurt and what I have coined *emotional astigmatism*. Just like this unnamed woman, many have blocked their blessings because the fault lines of their past obstructs their view. As we eavesdrop on their conversation, we can hear the master

Psychologist assess and expose her issues and faults by allowing her to speak. She struggled with the issues of race due to the conduct of society.

Again, don't block your blessing. She struggled with her faith seeking only natural means to get aid. She struggled with her perception, and she struggled with her thirst. She realized that she was thirsty for something that natural water could not provide. And finally, when she realized her thirst, our Lord so masterfully pointed out His issues. She was married four times and now she had a *whatchamacallit*. Jesus was there not only to diagnose, but also to heal her, so that He could use her flaws and turn them into strength. She immediately dropped her pots and ran to the city and truly evangelized until the men of the city came and the Gospel was spread in Samaria.

Yes, our God can and will heal you and make you whole. He knows where to find you and knows how deep your fault lines run. She went from mess and misery to having a message and a mission. Hallelujah! Even now, I sense in my spirit that God will heal you as you read this book, so that you can help others, by moving from blocking your blessing due to bitterness to being a blessing by the grace of God.

Unattended fault-lines can also hinder your Kingdom ministry. We see it in the life of Jonah. He received a mighty assignment from God to evangelize Nineveh, but refused and went in another direction. A storm arose. I hear the Lord say there is a message and a lesson in your storm. And as you can recall, He became fish bait for three miraculous days. But because God is a God of mercy, He gave him another chance. Thus, he fulfilled his assigned preaching for three days. The people were delivered yet Jonah was bitter until God exposed him and revealed his deficiency of grace.

"So Jonah went out of the city, and sat on the east side of the city, and there made him a booth, and sat under it in the shadow, till he might see what would become of the city. And the LORD God prepared a gourd, and made it to come up over Jonah, that it might be a shadow over his head, to deliver him from his grief. So Jonah was exceeding glad of the gourd. But God prepared a worm when the morning rose the next day, and it smote the gourd that it withered. And it came to pass, when the sun did arise, that God prepared a vehement east wind; and the sun beat upon the head of Jonah, that he fainted, and wished in himself to die, and said, It is better for me to die than to live.

And God said to Jonah, Doest thou well to be angry for the gourd? And he said, I do well to be angry, even unto death. Then said the LORD, Thou hast had pity on the gourd, for the which thou hast not laboured, neither madest it grow; which came up in a night, and perished in a night: And should not I spare Nineveh, that great city, wherein are more than sixscore thousand persons that cannot discern between their right hand and their left hand; and also much cattle?" Jonah 4:5-11.

What a powerful example of how we can preach and teach others but yet there are issues within that cause us to judge whether or not others should be blessed with grace. Thus, we block our own blessings. Yet, there is victory in Jesus. He specializes not in fault finding, but *healing those dangerous fault lines*.

Chapter 14

The Grace to Erase and Power to Overcome!

14

The Grace to Erase and Power to Overcome!

"For whatsoever is born of God overcometh the world: and this is the victory that overcometh the world, even our faith."
1 John 5:4

Now, you may ask, "How do I overcome personal fault and dangerous fault-lines? How do I erase the matters of the heart that have hindered me for so long? First, you must acknowledge. Secondly, you must submit to the One who is capable of releasing you and renewing you to a state of peace.

In John chapter 8, we have discussed a unique situation whereby a woman has been presented before the Master by those who had ulterior motives. The scene was one of such that she was snatched in the very act of adultery, indicted in the eyes of her accusers, and brought before our Lord. Her case was being tried in the Temple. Isn't it amazing how we can experience judgment in places of refuge by those anointed to help? But what they did in their vile and unsavory actions positioned her before the only One capable of truly forgiving her. And after our Lord so skillfully addressed them, He stood alone before her. Listen to His statement:

*"When Jesus had lifted up himself, and saw none but the woman, he said unto her, Woman, where are those thine accusers? hath no man condemned thee? She said, No man, Lord. And Jesus said unto her, **Neither do I condemn thee**: go, and sin no more"* John 8:10,11.

Jesus is the only One who flawlessly sits in the seat of judgment. The only One who could rightfully judge her. But yet He expressed grace. He was without fault. But yet He showed grace. Listen to the words of Pilate when he was cross-examined Himself as He stood trial.

*"Then said Pilate to the chief priests and to the people, I find **no fault** in this man"* Luke 23:4.

Now, let's take a look at how He dealt with our offenses.

"I, even I, am he that blotteth out thy transgressions for mine own sake, and will not remember thy sins" Isaiah 43:25.

The Hebrew word translated "blot out" in Psalm 51 means to abolish, destroy, **erase**, or utterly wipe away, according to Strong's Concordance:

*"Now to **erase** means to remove all traces of (thoughts, feelings, or memory). When we consider this, it seems to be illogical, nonsensical, even absurd. But where man sees impossibilities God again demonstrates the power of his grace. He alone is qualified to teach us the ultimate power of forgiveness and how to grace covers."*

Unlike today, I grew up during a time when lessons and instructions were written on a chalkboard. The first day of school, the board would look pristine with only a few instructions such as your teacher's name. I never considered anything much at that time until the end of the school year. Myself and two of my classmates were asked to come to school and help our teachers prepare for the summer. One of our assignments was to clean the chalkboard. She instructed us to get a bucket of warm water wherein she added vinegar and with a little effort, we cleaned the chalk boards removing all the residue from a year of teaching. Now, the eraser did a fine job but to really clean it demanded what we called elbow grease, or greater effort. Praise be unto God that His grace leaves no residual evidence of our faults! And now, it is our responsibility to follow His example.

*"As every man hath received the gift, even so **minister the same** one to another, as good stewards of the manifold grace of God"* 1 Peter 4:10.

"Frequently, the enemy entices Christians to harbor an unforgiving spirit—a very common symptom indeed among God's children. Such bitterness and fault-finding and enmity inflict a severe blow upon spiritual life." — **Watchman Nee**

Notice, the grace we have received is a gift but the administration of such divine grace to others is a service that will cost us. It cannot be stated enough the power of God's grace! It brings peace, strengthens weakness, and even covers a multitude of offenses. We are cautioned not to go on a fault finding mission in others but rather remain cognizant of the faults we were forgiven of. Then, we can have true liberty and live a guilt and regret free life.

The grace of God has liberated you and rather than being a victim of past experiences, seeking to place the blame on others. Which I realize that it is valid and just. Choose to be free of your past hurt and not allow the pain of your past to be a present prison. Victory in Christ is yours! He has delivered you and removed the charges and erased all residue. Not only has He healed you; now, you are whole. Your life is a testament of how you can overcome what once overwhelmed you. You are a written epistle, an open book, a sign and a wonder.

Woman of God, you are the original Wonder Woman!

"I am as a wonder unto many; but thou art my strong refuge" Psalm 71:7.

Man of God, you are the original Super Man!

"So God created man in his own image, in the image of God created he him; male and female created he them" Genesis 1:27.

Group Session
Guidelines and Exercises

Group Session
Guidelines and Exercises

Keys to conquering when internal fault lines are discovered:

Now that we have identified the multiple fault lines in our own lives, how do we address them?

1.   We should all have a confidant that we trust and feel free to be naked and not ashamed of. One who gives Godly counsel and one who prays with and for us. Who is that person in your life?

*"Confess your **faults** one to another, and pray one for another, that ye may be healed. The effectual fervent prayer of a righteous man availeth much"* James 5:16.

"Open rebuke is better than secret love. Faithful are the wounds of a friend; but the kisses of an enemy are deceitful" Proverb 27:5,6.

2.   We have learned that harboring offenses can create fault lines. We cannot control the remorse or repentance of those who have caused the offense. But yet we can choose to forgive. One

of the practices that works for me when an apology never comes, I write the apology for them and respond by saying:

I forgive you and release you of the debt of peace that you have caused due to our misunderstanding.

3.   Release yourself because your faults have been forgiven. Trust in the grace of God for your liberty. Your pass must be placed in its proper position. That's behind you. If you see through the lens of God, you will find that only goodness and mercy follows you.

4.   Seek trusted **spiritual counsel** that you can give account-ability to. One whom you can be totally transparent and one that you respect.

5.   The Bible teaches us when confronting any situation, it requires courage, faith, and grace. All of which should be adapted in your process.

6.   Surrender to the Power of God and be free.

Let us Pray:

Precious Father, we humbly come before You with an attitude of gratitude for the wonderful opportunity that You have afforded us to commune with You in prayer. Thank You for allowing us to be instruments of love by extended grace and forgiveness to those who have offended us. We now recognize our responsibility as Your sons and daughters. And therefore, we choose freedom over debt.

Father, You have forgiven us and therefore we choose to exemplify the same Christian character as Your child and now release others of their debt of offense. We praise You for counting us worthy of this endeavor and desire to be pleasing to You in all that we do.

May Your love continue to be shed abroad through us by Your Holy Spirit. And may we continue to be pleasing to You in all we say and do. These wonderful blessings we ask in the name of Your Son, Jesus Christ.

Meet the Author

D r. Frank A. Jones, III is the Pastor and Founder of *City of Refuge Ministries* in White Castle, Louisiana. He is the husband of Felisha Nelson Jones for 32 years and the father of three amazing kids Raven, Stephen, and Bryanna Jones. Along with three wonderful grandkids. He is an accomplished Pastor, preacher, and teacher whose ministry has spanned more than three decades.

As a Kingdom gift, his ministry has impacted lives globally. He is renowned for his counsel to many sons and daughters in the faith as well as generations of civic leaders. He believes that all the cures to society's ills can be found in the Word of God, and that true Victory and Success begins from within.

Bibliography

[i] *Feeling Good: The New Mood of Therapy Cognitive Behavior*. Burns, M.D. David D. William Morrow & Company. New York City, NY. 1999.

[ii] "That disaster happened along the New Madrid Seismic Zone in southeast Missouri in late 1811 and early 1812 when three mammoth quakes occurred over several days," Brian Houser of Quake Kare in St. Louis.

[iii] https://patch.com/missouri/universitycity/earthquake-changed-course-mississippi-river.

www.ingramcontent.com/pod-product-compliance
Lightning Source LLC
Chambersburg PA
CBHW072054150726
47999CB00005B/1775